Introduction

The Ladybird Key Words Picture Dictionary is designed to promote children's rapid learning of English.

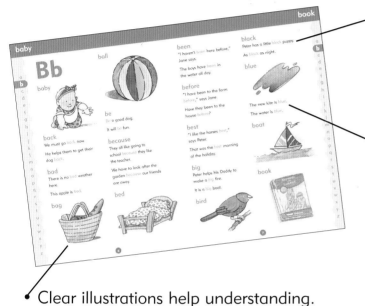

The example sentences come from the Key Words reading scheme, ensuring their simplicity and relevance to the reader.

Two simple sentences are used to show the meaning and usage of each word.

• Subject-based word lists at the back of the book will help with writing for projects or on a particular theme.

• Clear illustrations help understanding.

Using this Dictionary

• Encourage the reader to find the word he needs and to look at the picture, or read the sentences.

• Look at how the word is used in the sentence. Can it be used in more than one way?

• When he has read the sentence several times, check if he can spell the word.

• Encourage the reader to write the sentences and to use the words in spoken and written work.

• Extend children's vocabulary and comprehension by talking about the sentences and illustrations.

• Use the themed pages to assist children's spoken and written work.

• It is especially helpful and motivating if this dictionary is used in conjunction with the Key Words Reading Scheme.

a
b
c
d
e
f
g
h
i
j
k
l
m
n
o
p
q
r
s
t
u
v
w
x
y
z

Aa

a

Here is a shop.

Peter sees a man and a boy.

about

The children talk about the farm.

It is about three o'clock in the afternoon.

after

We must run after our boats.

Run after him, Peter.

afternoon

It is very hot this afternoon.

The two children sit in the afternoon sun.

again

Here they come again.

The sun is out again.

always

We always have tea at five o'clock.

You are always a good dog.

all

All children like to read.

The children, Daddy and Mummy all go to the sea.

am

I am not too hot.

I am going to take the dog for a walk.

an

Here is an apple tree.

Peter has an apple, and Jane has an apple.

and

Here are Peter and Jane.

The boys and girls go to school.

another

Do you want another apple?

Mummy and Daddy talk to one another.

any

Have you any money?

I can not walk any more.

apple

are

Peter and Jane are at home.

Here are some cakes.

as

We must go home now as it is one o'clock.

They talk to the men as they fish.

ask

They ask him to help.

We must ask them first.

at

Look at me.

They look at the rabbits.

away

They put the play things away.

The dog runs away.

a
b
c
d
e
f
g
h
i
j
k
l
m
n
o
p
q
r
s
t
u
v
w
x
y
z

a
b
c
d
e
f
g
h
i
j
k
l
m
n
o
p
q
r
s
t
u
v
w
x
y
z

Bb

baby

back

We must go back now.

He helps them to get their dog back.

bad

There is no bad weather here.

This apple is bad.

bag

ball

be

Be a good dog.

It will be fun.

because

They all like going to school because they like the teacher.

We have to look after the garden because our friends are away.

bed

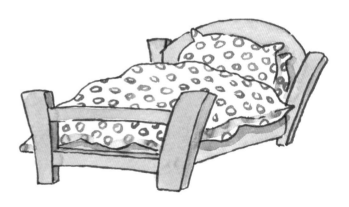

been

"I haven't been here before," Jane says.

The boys have been in the water all day.

before

"I have been to the farm before," says Jane.

Have they been to the house before?

best

"I like the horses best," says Peter.

That was the best morning of the holiday.

big

Peter helps his Daddy to make a big fire.

It is a big boat.

bird

black

Peter has a little black puppy.

As black as night.

blue

The new kite is blue.

The water is blue.

boat

book

Keywords with Ladybird

a
b
c
d
e
f
g
h
i
j
k
l
m
n
o
p
q
r
s
t
u
v
w
x
y
z

box

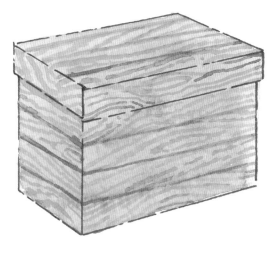

bus

boy

Peter is a boy.

The boy is going to the shop.

bring

"May we bring the dog?" asks Aunty.

The sea brings things in.

brother

Peter is Jane's brother.

but

The children look in the toy shops but they do not go in.

"Pat can come in," says Daddy, "but he must be a good dog."

buy

Aunty sends the children out to buy ice-creams.

"I've been to buy you a present," says Uncle.

by

"I like to go by the farm," says Peter.

They like to go by train.

Cc

café

They find the café and go in.

They have ice-cream at the café.

cake

call

Peter calls Jane and Aunty.

"I call this picture, 'My Day'," says Jane.

came

"The donkey came last week," Jane tells Peter.

Two men came up the road this morning.

can

Jane can make ice-cream.

Can you see the train?

can't

"I can't get the balloon," says Bob.

"We can't go without the dog," says Peter.

cap

car

cat

a b c d e f g h i j k l m n o p q r s t u v w x y z

chair

children

The children are in the tree.

The dog is with the children.

Christmas

closed

The door is closed.

The box is closed.

come

The children know their holiday will come to an end.

Peter comes down from the tree.

could

"I could make some ice-cream," says Jane.

"I wish we could go on the pier," says Peter.

cow

cup

Dd

day

They play games every day.

She tells Mary about the day by the sea.

Daddy

They help Daddy with the car.

Daddy and Peter have some water.

danger

There is no danger.

"I can read, DANGER, STOP," says Peter.

dear

"What a dear little dog!" says Jane.

Dear Jane and Peter,
It's time to write you a letter.

did

"Did you get your kite?" asks Aunty.

"We did have fun there," says Peter.

dig

"I will dig the garden," says Daddy.

"Help me dig this up," says Jane.

dinner

do

The children can do what they like.

"What do you want?" she asks.

dog

a
b
c
d
e
f
g
h
i
j
k
l
m
n
o
p
q
r
s
t
u
v
w
x
y
z

doll

don't

"We don't want to get wet,"
says Peter.

"Don't run," says Mary.

door

down

Up and down we go!

Peter puts his toys down.

draw

"I will draw a tree,"
says Peter.

The children like to draw.

drink

A drink of water.

The baby chicks have
to learn how to eat
and drink.

Ee

eat

"Eat up your eggs," says Mother.

We eat our dinner at five o'clock.

egg

end

Peter and Jane are at the end of the pier.

It is the end of the holiday.

entrance

ENTRANCE THIS WAY

every

They put every pencil in the box.

The children go to the farm every day.

EXIT

"EXIT means the way out," says Peter.

"That says EXIT," says Jane.

EXIT

a b c d e **f** g h i j k l m n o p q r s t u v w x y z

Ff

farm

The children are at the farm.

The children like the farm animals.

fast

Peter runs fast with the kite.

The motor boat is going very fast.

father

fell

She fell down in the garden.

The tent fell down once more.

first

"You go first," says Jane.

"We must ask them first," says Peter.

fish

find

Bob finds some eggs.

They look into the water to find some fish.

fire

five

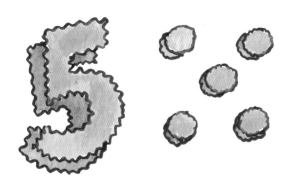

All five get in the motor boat.

"It is five o'clock," says Aunty.

flower

fly

The birds fly away.

"Can we fly the kite," says Jane.

for

"This is for you," Jane says.

"Here is some water for you, Peter," says Aunty.

four

"It is four o'clock," says Jane.

"There are four of us," says Peter. We want four seats in the boat."

found

"We found just what we wanted," says Jane.

The children have found the toy shop.

from

"Here is a letter from Mum," calls out Jane.

The children come out to buy ice-creams from the man in the van.

fun

"It is fun," says Jane, "we like this."

It is fun to play games.

a
b
c
d
e
f
g
h
i
j
k
l
m
n
o
p
q
r
s
t
u
v
w
x
y
z

Gg

game

They talk about the game they will play.

The two children like to play games.

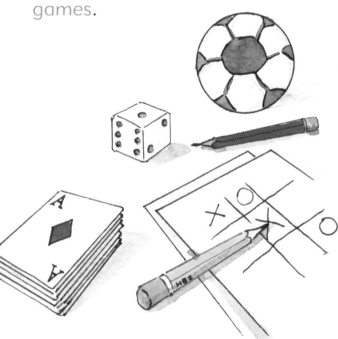

gave

Bob gave his sister a bag of sweets.

Jane's brother gave them some apples.

get

"Get in the boat," says Peter.

"Get some flowers, Peter," says Jane.

girl

Jane is a girl.

give

"Give the rabbit some water," says Jane.

"Can we give apples to the horses?" asks Peter.

go

"We will go up the hill,"
says Daddy.

The dog wants to go in the water.
"Let him go," says Daddy.

got

Dad got in the car
to help to find the
puppy.

"I have got five toys,"
says Peter.

going

The dog is going after
the rabbits.

The afternoon sun is
going down.

green

The garden is green.

"I like green apples best,"
says Jane.

good

"This will be a good house
for us to play in," says Peter.

"These apples are good,"
says Jane.

Hh

a
b
c
d
e
f
g
h
i
j
k
l
m
n
o
p
q
r
s
t
u
v
w
x
y
z

had

"We have had our tea," says Peter.

"We can see the hill where we had our walk," says Jane.

half

It is half past three in the afternoon.

"Please give me half an apple," says Peter.

hand

Peter has his boat in his hand.

She has a doll in her hand.

has

Peter has a toy.

Jane has a look.

hat

have

The children have sweets and toys.

"We have to go," says Peter.

he

The boy runs up and he jumps into the water.

"Here you are Jane," he says.

head

help

Jane and Peter like to help.

"Help me," says Pam.

her

Jane puts her fish into the water.

Jane wants to keep her little horse.

here

Here is Peter and here is Jane.

"Come here Pat," says
Peter. "Be a good dog."

hill

him

"The man likes us to help
him with his work," says Peter.

"Here is the toy dog," says
Jane. "Put him with the toy
horses."

his

Peter is at work with his Daddy.

Peter puts his big fish into
the water.

home

"I want to go home," says Jane.
"This is my home."

horse

hot

It is a hot day again.

The water is hot.

house

how

Peter knows how to read.
Jane shows them how to
cook.

a b c d e f g **h** i j k l m n o p q r s t u v w x y z

19

Ii

I

I like Peter and I like Jane.

"Look Jane," says Peter,
"I can jump."

if

"If the rabbits see us,
they will go," says Peter.

Jane can go to Mary's
house if she wants to.

in

Peter is in the toy shop.

The fish is in the water.

ink

into

Jane and Peter jump into
the water.

The children go into the
sweet shop.

is

Here is Peter and here is
Jane.

Is the dog here?

it

It is fun in the water.

The train comes in.
"Look at it," says
Peter.

Jj

jam

jump

They jump in the water.

"Can you jump like this?" says Peter.

just

"Just let me have a go with the kite," says Jane.

"We found just what we wanted," says Peter.

Kk

keep

"Keep the dog away from the fire," says Daddy.

"We will always keep the book," says Mother.

know

Peter and Jane know the policeman.

Peter and Jane know how to read.

kite

a
b
c
d
e
f
g
h
i
j
k
l
m
n
o
p
q
r
s
t
u
v
w
x
y
z

Ll

last

"I had some ice-cream last week," said Jane.

"That is the last cake," says Pam.

laugh

The children laugh and have fun with the camera.

Peter laughs at an old photograph.

learn

Our teacher helps us to learn to read.

"Do you want to learn to swim?" says Mummy.

left

I left my hat in the garden.

There is plenty of room left in the boat.

let

"Let the dog go," says Daddy.

"Will you let me help, please?" says Jane.

letter

like

I like the toy shop.

"I can make cakes like Mummy," says Jane.

little

Jane has two little fish.

Jane has a little boat and Peter has a big boat.

live

"This is where the horses live," says Pam.

Pam likes to live on the farm.

long

Peter and Jane talk about their long summer holiday.

"You have been a long time," says Pam.

look

"Come and look," says Jane.

"Do I look very old?" says Peter.

lost

The puppy ran away and was lost all day.

"I have lost the game," says Peter.

love

They all love to play in the garden.

The two children love their grandmother and grandfather.

a
b
c
d
e
f
g
h
i
j
k
l
m
n
o
p
q
r
s
t
u
v
w
x
y
z

Mm

made

They made a cake with Daddy.

I have made a nice tea for you.

make

"Let us make a house in the tree," says Peter.

I will make the tea.

man

many

Many children are in the water.

If it rains, not many children buy ice-creams.

may

"May we bring the dog?" asks Aunty.

"May we have tea for two?" asks Uncle.

me

"Look at me," says Peter.

Here is a cake for you and a cake for me.

men

I can see the men.

The men will put out the fire.

milk

money

more

"You can have some more apples," says Mummy.

"Can we see more of the farm?" asks Peter.

morning

The next morning, Peter tells his aunty and uncle about the boat.

"That was the best morning of the holidays," says Peter.

mother

"The eggs are for you," says Pam's mother to Jane.

The two girls buy some flowers for their mothers.

Mr

Mr Green is by his car.

"I will help you," says Mr Green.

Mrs

Mrs Green talks to Jane's mother.

Mary looks after Molly if Mrs Green is not there.

much

She does not do much work.

Mr and Mrs Green like Jane very much.

Mummy

Jane and Peter like to help Mummy.

"Let us all go home for tea," says Mummy.

must

"He must be a good dog," says Daddy.

"I must have some tea," says Mummy.

my

"Look at my big fish," says Peter.

"Away I go on my horse," says Jane.

a
b
c
d
e
f
g
h
i
j
k
l
m
n
o
p
q
r
s
t
u
v
w
x
y
z

Nn

name

"What is the name of the yellow flowers?" says Peter.

The children write their names.

never

The children have never had a kite.

"I have never been there before," says Aunty.

new

The motor boat is new.

"Here is some money to buy a new kite," says Uncle.

next

The family live next door to the farm.

"I want to go on a donkey next," says Peter.

nice

It is nice to see you again.

"He is a nice little dog," says Peter.

night

no

"No apples for you, Pat," says Peter.

"Will you keep the fish?" "No," says Peter.

not

Peter can not stop the cat.

That is not Daddy's car.

nothing

I have nothing to do.

Jane calls Peter, but hears nothing.

now

Can we go now?

Pam says, "Now we will look at the horses."

Oo

o'clock

"We must go home now as
it is one o'clock," says Uncle.

It is three o'clock in the afternoon.

of

Jane gives the little pigs
some of her cake.

They can see the top of the hill.

off

"Get off, Pat," says Peter.
"Be a good dog."

The children get off the bus,
then they go off to the shops.

old

Grandmother is old, like
Grandfather.

They live in an old house.

on

"Come on," says Peter.
"Come on the boat."

Jane looks on.

one

It is one o'clock.

"This is the one we want,"
says Jane.

once

"We will play once more,"
says Jane.

They go for help at once.

only

She is the only one who
looks after the garden.

There is only one butterfly.

open

She opens the door
and goes in.

The shop is open.

or

They can play games, or fish, or
be with Mummy and Daddy.

"You or I will get the cat,"
says Peter.

a
b
c
d
e
f
g
h
i
j
k
l
m
n
o
p
q
r
s
t
u
v
w
x
y
z

a b c d e f g h i j k l m n **o** p q r s t u v w x y z

other

Who is the other man
in the train?

"Not this bus," says Mummy.
"We want the other one."

our

"Those children go to our
school," says Jane.

"We have had our tea,"
says Peter.

out

Mummy looks out of the
window.

"It is time to go out," says
Daddy.

over

The dog runs fast over the
sands and into the water.

"Come over here," says
Jane.

own

Mary has her own doll.

Their aunty and uncle have
no children of their own.

Pp

pen

pencil

people

Some people are going to the
water.

You will soon learn like other
people.

picture

Peter finds a picture he likes.

"Would they like a picture?"

pig

place

"This is a nice place for a picnic," says Aunty.

This place is good for playing in.

play

Jane and Peter play in the water.

"Let us put the play things away," says Mummy.

please

"I want two tickets please," says Peter.

"Please can I help you to make a cake," says Jane.

Police

PRIVATE

They see a door which has PRIVATE on it.

Peter says, "It has PRIVATE on it so that children will not go in."

pull

"Pat is going down after the rabbits," says Mummy. "Pull him out, Peter."

They pull out the chairs and sit down.

push

"Push the toy car quickly," says Jane.

"We can put the tent up," says Peter. "You push this, and I will pull."

put

"Let us put the play things away," says Mummy.

Peter puts his books down.

a
b
c
d
e
f
g
h
i
j
k
l
m
n
o
p
q
r
s
t
u
v
w
x
y
z

Qq

queen

quickly

Jane skips quickly.

Peter learns quickly.

Rr

rabbit

rain

ran

The puppy ran away and was lost all day.

They ran over the sands.

read

"All children like to read,"
says Peter.

"Read this," says Jane.

red

The man in the shop
has the red apples the
children like.

It is fun in the red bus.

right

"That's not the right
way to fly the kite,"
says Peter.

"It is the right day for
a picnic," says Uncle.

road

They go fast along the road.

This is a good road.

room

round

They ran round so much
that they got very hot.

She looks round the
garden.

run

Pat runs after the rabbits
and Peter runs after Pat.

The children run races.

Ss

said

He said Jane could use it.

"The man at the farm said we can go there again."

sat

Mum sat down in the sun.

The children sat in the garden.

saw

"We saw cows," says Jane.

They saw the big boat.

says

"It is fun in the water," says Peter.

Jane says she likes dogs.

school

They like school.

The boys and girls go to school.

sea

seat

see

Peter can see a fish in the water.

"We can see the rabbit we want," they say.

seen

The fire can be seen a long way away.

"They must have seen the boat," says Simon.

she

Jane helps Peter. "It looks good," she says.

"That will be fun," she says.

shop

Jane is in the toy shop.

"I like to shop", says Jane.

should

"Should we go home?" asks Peter.

"I should like a picnic in the woods," says Jane.

sing

"I like to sing," says Jane.

The birds sing in the trees.

sister

Peter and his sister get off the bus to walk home.

The brother and sister talk about their friends.

sit

"Sit down," says Jane.

They all sit down to eat.

slow

"You are too slow at this game," says Peter.

The donkey is slow.

so

"There are rabbits," says Peter. "I said so."

Pam likes to work at the farm so she can see the horses.

soon

"We will soon be home," says Mummy.

The children soon come to the station.

some

Peter has some water.

Some of the children play games.

station

The station is on this road.

Peter and Jane are at the station.

stop

"Stop the cat," says Jane.

The train will stop at the station.

street

They walk down the street.

The shop is in the street.

sun

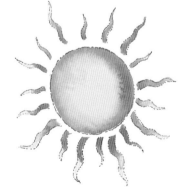

sweets

a
b
c
d
e
f
g
h
i
j
k
l
m
n
o
p
q
r
s
t
u
v
w
x
y
z

Tt

a
b
c
d
e
f
g
h
i
j
k
l
m
n
o
p
q
r
s
t
u
v
w
x
y
z

table

take

Peter takes the bag from Daddy.

"Daddy will take us by car," says Peter.

talk

Daddy talks to the man about the walk.

The children talk about the farm.

tea

tell

Mummy tells Peter to help Father with the bags.

Jane tells Mary about her friend Tom.

than

"I like colour better than black and white," says Peter.

"I like nothing better than a nice swim," says Mum.

thank

"Thank you for helping me," says Daddy.

Peter thanks Jane for the tea.

that

"We want that rabbit," says Peter.

Daddy says that he will play.

the

The train comes in.

Peter is in the tree.

their

The horses like their work.

The children eat their eggs.

them

Peter looks at the fish.
"I can see them," he says.

Jane gives them some of her cake.

then

The children get off the bus, then they go off to the shops.

"I will be the man in the shop," says Peter. "Then let me be Mummy, " Jane says.

there

"Look," says Peter. "There go the Police."

"I like to go there," says Jane.

these

"These clothes are just right for dressing up," says Peter.

"He can have fun with these things," says Jane.

they

Here they are.

They jump into the water for fun.

this

"This is for you," says Peter.

"We like this," they say.

thing

"I want to buy some things for tea," says Jane.

"Let us put the play things away," says Mummy.

think

"I think that was the best morning of the holiday, "says Peter.

"I think I would like an ice-cream, please," says Pam.

those

"We should have asked those men to help us," says Jane.

"The dog must be under those clothes," says Peter.

three

All three children like the horses.

It is three o'clock.

a
b
c
d
e
f
g
h
i
j
k
l
m
n
o
p
q
r
s
t
u
v
w
x
y
z

time

"What is the time?" asks Peter.

"It must soon be time to go home," says Jane.

to

The dog likes to jump.

The children go to the shop.

today

Today, Bob asks Peter to come out to play.

The sun is out today.

too

"It is a good road," says Mother, "and the man will not go too fast."

"Your uncle is on holiday, too," says Mother.

took

Peter took the book to his teacher.

Jane took the bat from Peter.

top

They can see the top of the hill.

Jane and Peter walk up to the top.

toy

"Look at the toy train," says Peter.

"Put the toys away now," says Mummy.

train

tree

two

Jane says, "I have two little fish."

It is two o'clock.

Uu

under

"I don't like it under the water," says Jane.

The dog is under the table.

up

"Jump up on the boat," says Peter.

They walk up to the top of the hill.

us

"Please let us draw," says Peter.

Jane says, "Daddy will help us make a house in a tree."

use

She tells them to use their pencils to draw.

"If you use things, you must put them away," says Pam.

Vv

van

very

Mary and Jane are very good friends.

Mr and Mrs Green like Jane very much.

a
b
c
d
e
f
g
h
i
j
k
l
m
n
o
p
q
r
s
t
u
v
w
x
y
z

a
b
c
d
e
f
g
h
i
j
k
l
m
n
o
p
q
r
s
t
u
v
w
x
y
z

walk

Come for a walk.

They walk by the water.

want

"I want to go home," says Jane.

The dog wants the fish.

was

"That was good," says Peter.

"I was walking to the farm," says Jane.

water

way

"Let me tell you the right way to fly the kite," he says.

"Come this way," says Peter.

we

"We like this," they say.

"We have to go," says Peter.

well

The toy boat is going well.

I hope that you are well.

went

Jane went to the farm.

We went into the barn to look for the puppy.

were

"We saw a boat when we were by the sea," says Jane.

"You were good to write the letters," says Aunty.

wet

Molly is wet.

"Don't get your hat wet," says Bob.

window

what

"What will you make," says Peter.

"What is that?" asks Jane.

when

Tom likes it best of all when he is in a boat.

"When is it time for tea?" asks Peter.

where

I like to go where there are trees and flowers.

"Where do you want to go, Peter?" says Mummy.

which

"Which station is this?" asks Jane.

"Which bag has the sweets?" asks Peter.

white

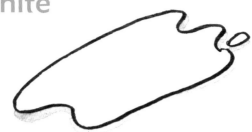

"Here is a white butterfly," says Pam.

Dad uses the white cap because of the sun.

who

Who is the other boy.

"The baby pigs know who looks after them," says Pam.

why

Why does Aunty call us?

Why not go on the pier now?

will

"Will you let me help you, please?" says Jane.

We will make some cakes.

with

Peter likes to play with toys.

Jane says, "Please can I play with you."

a
b
c
d
e
f
g
h
i
j
k
l
m
n
o
p
q
r
s
t
u
v
w
x
y
z

a
b
c
d
e
f
g
h
i
j
k
l
m
n
o
p
q
r
s
t
u
v
w
x
y
z

wish

"I wish we could go in the motor boat," says Peter.

They wish they could see Punch and Judy every day.

work

Peter helps Daddy work on the car.

"It is good to work, and it is good to play," says Mummy.

woman

would

"It would be nice if we could go out in the motor boat."

"Would you like to come, too?" asks Jane.

write

Peter says, "We will write letters to our friends."

They write very well.

x-ray

Peter has to go to hospital for an X-ray.

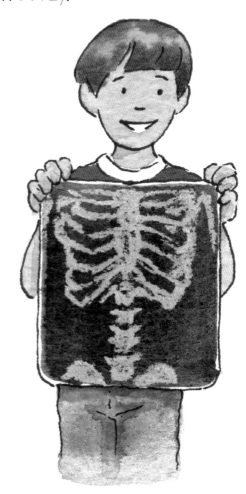

"What does my X-ray show?" Peter asks the doctor.

Yy

yes

Peter says, "Yes, we will."

"Do you like it in the water," asks Pam. "Yes," says Jane.

yellow

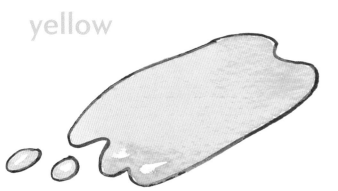

Pam looks at the little yellow chicks.

"Those yellow flowers are sunflowers," says Jane.

you

"I will give these apples to you," says Jane.

"Can you see the fire?" asks Peter.

Zz

zebra

zoo

Families

grandfather

dad/daddy

mum/mummy

aunty

uncle

grandmother

brother

sister

Food

bread

butter

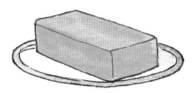

milk

cheese

eggs

banana

apple

potato

onion

carrot

lettuce

strawberry

tomato

orange

Body

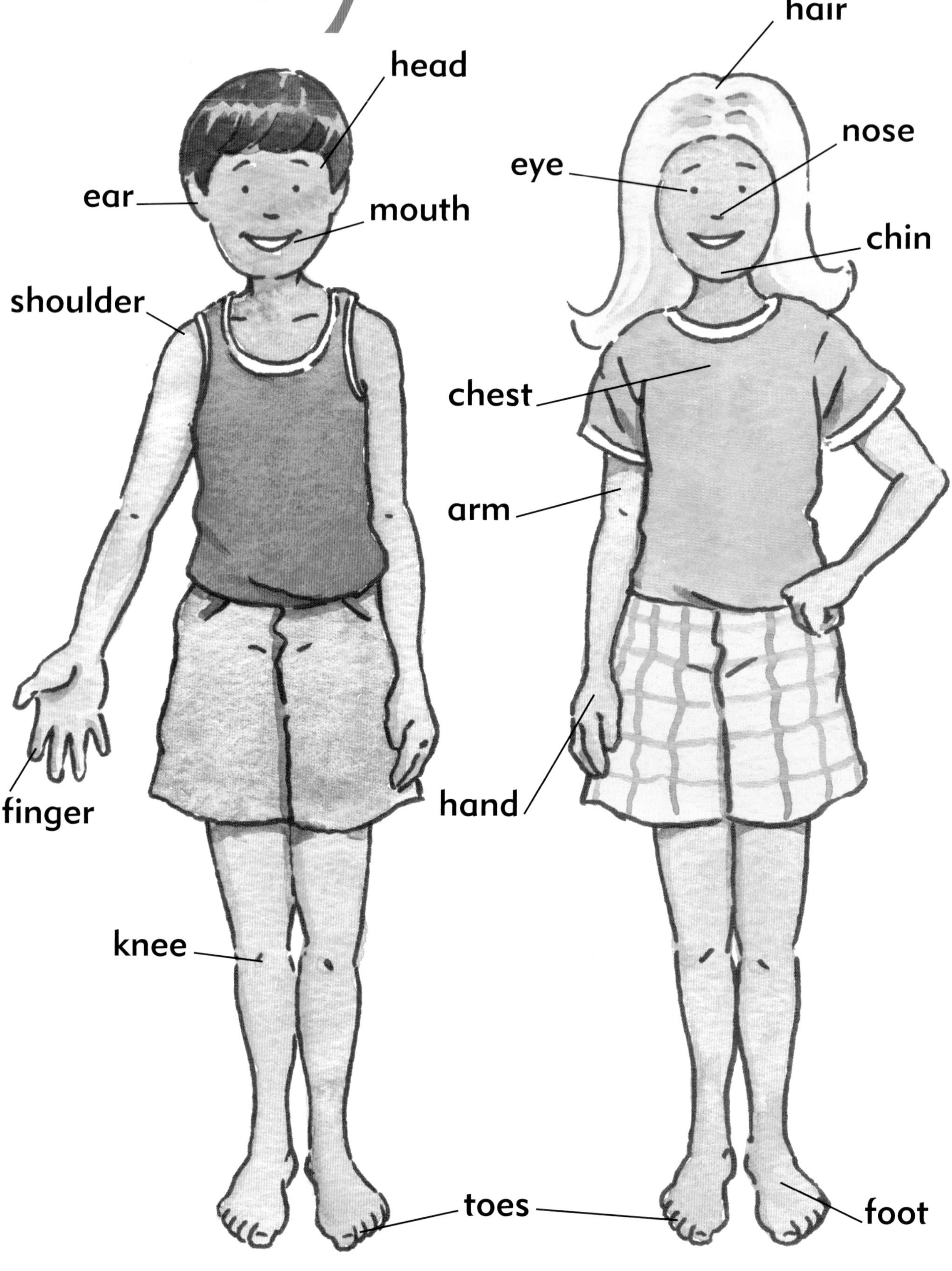

hair

head

eye

nose

ear

mouth

chin

shoulder

chest

arm

finger

hand

knee

toes

foot

44

Colours

red

brown

orange

black

yellow

white

green

pink

blue

grey

purple

Numbers

0 nought	**1** one	**2** two	**3** three	**4** four
5 five	**6** six	**7** seven	**8** eight	**9** nine
10 ten	**11** eleven	**12** twelve	**13** thirteen	**14** fourteen
15 fifteen	**16** sixteen	**17** seventeen	**18** eighteen	**19** nineteen

20 twenty	**30** thirty	**40** forty	**50** fifty	**60** sixty
70 seventy	**80** eighty	**90** ninety	**100** one hundred	

500 five hundred	**1000** one thousand	**1000 000** one million

Days

Sunday	Monday	Tuesday
Wednesday	Thursday	Friday
Saturday		

Months

January	February	March
April	May	June
July	August	September
October	November	December

Seasons

Spring	Summer
Autumn	Winter

Opposite words

above   below

up   down

begin   end

awake   asleep

top   bottom

open   closed

deep   shallow

even   odd

fast   slow

over   under